BY

JONTUE RICE

THE INSPIRATION FASHION,
Colors of Jesus' Soul

Copyright © 2023 Jontue Rice

All rights reserved.

ISBN:
9798861528597

Library of Control Number:
2023918069

Printed in the United States of America

First Edition, 2023

For information, write to the author:
Jontue Rice
jontuerice570@gmail.com

INTRODUCTION

"Even though I work with color, style and clothing every day, the power of color never ceases to amaze me. When we wear clothes that conceal that authentic self, we flourish. When we wear colors that conceal that authentic self, we flounder-even when we have the looks, talent and personality to succeed".

-David Zyla
Famous Costume Designer
Author: The Color of Style

People always see the true colors in all of us every day. Every wonderful fashion show I attended as a photographer, I saw the best in fashion designs, and the great craft of the designers. The important details of our lives is Color.

It was the designs, colors, and vibe that was so delightful and had brought a great vision among so many models and supporters.

The colors we surround ourselves in with can influence our perspectives and emotions. It helps us communicate both ideas and those emotions and can be used across industries to achieve results and define experiences.

Ultimately, colors help us navigate the world around us and add richness to our lives. Under the influence of different colors, we feel and think differently.

The Fashion industry had it advantages, disadvantages, challenges, and celebrations. Now-a-days it's about seeing how to stay fresh, immovable, always having a goal and having a mission.

The Greek for fashion is "Moda" which mean to trend and to style. The fashion designer must use wisdom, being culture-minded, having a vision and knowing what is acceptable.

I took a deeper look at the colors of each

fashion design. It was so amazing to be that there are colors that honor Jesus. The colors in the bible have a significance that can represent God and his plans for redemption. Just like with numbers, colors point us to Jesus by symbolizing his person and his works. It can also tell us the seasons.

God is a God of symbolism, and he speaks through symbolism. One of the ways is color. Colors do have meaning and of course, multiple ones. In this book, we well learn the colors of Jesus, why this symbolizing Jesus and what the color mean and represent.

Table of Contents

Chapter 1

RED

1John 1:7-9 says that but if we walk in the light, as he is in the light, we have fellowship one with another, and the blood of Jesus his Son cleanseth us from all sin.

Red represents the blood of Jesus shed for our sins, offering salvation to all. It also represents s love, passion, desire, heart, strength and leadership. Jesus Christ is the center of the color Red. The blood that died on that cross, created the New Testament and the new covenant with him.

The word "NEW" speaks for itself. Revelations 21:5 says, and he who was seated on the throne said, "Behold, I am making all things new." Also, he said, "Write this down, for these words are trustworthy and true."

No matter what you have done in the past. Let the Color of Red refresh, restore, and renew you. Let it make all things new in your life. What the devil created for evil with red, Gods created color made it for your good. 2 Corinthians 5:17 says Therefore, if anyone is in Christ, he is a new creation. The old has passed away; behold, the new has come.

There is something greater when you put on red because it suits the love of God. If you are a lover, if you are a person that have passions and desires, then the color Red looks good on you.

On a very nice a pleasant day no matter whether it is a dress, skirt, shirt, pants, or even a suit, wear it and walk like you are brand new and filled with boldness. The past doesn't determine you character God does. That's the principle that you want to have when you see the color red. Think of that color as new beginnings. Rethink, Reinterpret, and Reimagine.

Chapter 2

ORANGE

Hebrews 12:28-29 says, Therefore, since we receive a kingdom which cannot be shaken, let us show gratitude, by which we may offer to God an acceptable service with reverence and awe; for our God is a consuming fire. The wording "Consuming Fire" is what I come out of my lips when I see the color Orange.

Orange means joy, warmth, enthusiasm, creativity, success, encouragement, determination, and change.

It is interesting that, Orange has one of

the strongest measurable physical effects of any color. Orange stimulates the appetite, increase energy level, and even stimulates the thyroid to boost metabolism.

Orange is powerful, and we can't ignore it, which explains why people have such marked reactions to it.

Job is clear that we all are not exempt from being tried in the fire. According to Job 23:10 it shares that he knows the way I take when he hath tried me, I shall come forth as gold.

Heat is very important. After using the crushers to reduce the ore to small gravel-sized pieces. These pieces go into drums with steel balls where they are ground to a fine powder.

Next, water is added to make it slurry which becomes a pulp. This pulp then goes into leaching tanks. Here the gold is chemically extracted with cyanide and oxygen.

A very messy process. it finally goes into the smelter at 2100-degree Fahrenheit. That's hot. But the gold isn't pure yet. It still needs refining. Refining is the necessary process that takes the impurities out of gold making it valuable and functional.

The unwanted elements are removed by melting the gold again with borax and soda ash, which is added to separate the pure gold from the lesser metals. This typically gives you 99.9% pure gold which is cast into bars.

It's all about allowing God to mold and make you so that you can be Pure as Gold". It's a mess and sometimes the process has to be repeat itself.

The purpose is coming to terms that we are more valuable than our comfort zone. It takes acknowledging our unprofessional methods and unacceptable behaviors. Presentation is key.

The question is this, 'Are you willing to ignite the fire that is in you to become excellent or are you just satisfied with being lukewarm?

There is no playing church here. God wants us to deal with the issues of sin. He does not want us to run any longer.

Change is a process. It's about putting together a strategy that will help you overcome the circumstances.

I can tell you that there are times when I am being put in the fire. But in that fire, I am becoming pure in my relationships and importantly my relationship with God.

Let's not get upset and offended when we are tried in the fire. Think of this, God want us to go into another level, but we must pass the test. That test in the fire.

Let's do a little research. First let's evaluate the word "Excellence". Excellence is defined as the quality of being outstanding or extremely good. In fact, the word *"Excel"* means to do or be better than or surpass.

Philippians 4:8 states, *'Finally, brothers, whatever is true, whatever is honorable, whatever is just, whatever is pure, whatever is lovely, whatever is commendable, if there is any excellence, if there is anything worthy of praise, think about these things.'*

God in our lives, so that we can understand the importance of studying to show thyself approved (2 Tim 2:15), be quick to hear, slow to speak, slow to anger (James 1:9), Letting the conversations be always full of grace, seasoned with salt (Colossians 4:6), and not to turn your back on wisdom (Proverbs 4:6).

So now you understand the efforts it takes to be excellent. Somebody reading this book will have to go back to school, take anger management or mental health courses or domestic violent classes, get a better job, needing a mentor or just take responsibility.

There is nothing wrong with saying I screwed up, I need help, I messed up, I made a mistake, or just admitting to your failures. Either way you are igniting the fire to be shaped to a greater character.

Eight years ago, as I made a mission to restore my relationship with Christ. I was pursuing to move forward, even in my marriage. Unfortunately, that didn't happen.

There were some things the holy spirit made clear to me that I have to manage and deal with. I felt that God was punishing me.

But I was reminded of a scripture in Psalms 31:24 that says be strong and take heart, all of you who hope in the Lord.

Take heart means to be courageous; to gain one's courage. Its knowing Christ victory overshadows all troubles.

Ask yourself; are u sensitive to criticism? are u easy to get offended? are you coachable? are you willing to take a stroke or two? It's easy to get satisfied and comfortable as far as status. But rest assured, that might not get you anywhere.

God wants to take the necessary steps to be successful in many proportions. Think of Orange as a goal seeker, a legacy maker, a world changer, an overcomer that is bold to take risks and not accept defeat or declaring failure.

When you put on Orange you are putting on pure fire. Think of it the new black. Enough said!

Chapter 3

YELLOW

1 John 1:5-7 This is the message we have heard from Him and announce to you, that God is Light, and in Him there is no darkness at all. If we say that we have fellowship with Him and yet walk in the darkness, we lie and do not practice the truth; but if we walk in the Light as He Himself is in the Light, we have fellowship with one another, and the blood of Jesus His Son cleanses us from all sin.

If we say that we have no sin, we are deceiving ourselves and the truth is not in us. If we confess our sins, He is faithful and righteous to forgive us our sins and to cleanse us from all unrighteousness. If we say that we have not sinned, we make Him a liar and His word is not in us.

Yellow means hope, happiness, freshness, positivity, clarity, energy, optimism, enlightenment, remembrance, and honor. Enough said. With light you can see reality, can make clear decisions and choices, follow direction wisely, and most importantly Grow. Think of it as a new awakening or new horizon or just Heaven.

My old Pastor had shared about having heavenly thoughts. In Colossians 3:1-4, Paul takes his time to focus on the mind and why blame him, the issue is wisdom. Dr. Mike Murdock says it clear "Every Problem is a Wisdom Problem". The greatest and only weapon the enemy can use against you is Ignorance.

Colossians 3:1-4 says Since then, you have been raised with Christ, set your hearts on things above, where Christ is seated at the right hand of God. Set your mind on the things above, not on earthly things. For you died, and your life is now hidden with Christ in God. When Christ, who is your life, appears, then you also will appear with him in glory.

The good things that happens when you have a positive attitude is that it enhances your motivation when carrying out tasks and working on goals, and you are also able to inspire and motivate others. It also creates an environment that is positive, healthy and uplifting.

As I was driving, I was thinking about how bad we have gotten with our tongue. Proverbs 18:21 says, "death and life are in the power of the tongue." The tongue is a small member of the body, but it is powerful. What we say to others can cut them to pieces or it can be a healing.

No matter what how u want your worldview is going to depend on how healthy your mouth is. We will go deeper in Chapter 4.

Imagine Heaven. Let's come to term of our new home how peaceful and how glorious it is. Nation will not take up sword against nation, nor will they train for war anymore" (Micah 4:3).

If you are a person that embrace peace or reconciliation, if you are a person with a gentle humble spirit or turn the other cheek, a person that is willing to forgive, or speak life, then yellow will be you attire.

My heart goes out to the community leaders, demonstrators, protesters and activists everywhere who is carrying the yellow spirit. Thank you for continually making a content effort into bringing peace and justice in many urban neighborhoods across the United States and around the world.

Chapter 4

GREEN

John 3:16 says for God so loved the world, that he gave his only Son, that whoever believes in him should not perish but have eternal life. Eternal Life with Jesus, Eternal Life period. Green mean's life, renewal, nature, growth, harmony, and freshness.

Did you know that from spinach to broccoli, green vegetables are the dynasty of good important nutritious diet. For years there have been positive research about the benefits of eating green. The truth is this, eating green vegetables:

- Helps the body burn fat.

- Helps your Cardiovascular system

- Help you burn fat and calories

- Help fight diabetes

- Provides sun protection

- Protects against toxins

Let us not talk about food let us talk about life, period. We need to ask ourselves are we doing it in vain. Is the things we doing is manifesting or turning into dust? Sometimes I sit back and think about the jobs I had, the people I had interacted with, the places I went, and the things I had done. I said to myself, "was it all in vain?" Maybe you were like me in that situation, it's not a bad thing. Sometimes you have to evaluate yourself.

No matter what you doing, how good or educated you are, if what you doing is hurting your relationship with God or destroying your life, if it is not prospering or enhancing your harvest nor producing fruit. Is what you doing is not allowing you to be a great person, or a better spouse than its time to refresh yourself or I can say "freshen up".

You want everything you are doing not only to last but also to set a legacy for your children. It starts with getting your life in order with God.

Now from what we are doing to what we say. We can be life builders or destroyers. Proverbs 18:21 it tells us that death and life are in the power of the tongue, and those who love it will eat its fruits. Think of this, the most important part of our body today can make or break anyone.

Let's talk about the weapons of personal destruction.

Gossip: Rumor or talk of a personal, sensational or intimate nature.

Rumor: Unverified information of uncertain origin usually spread by word of mouth or hearsay.

Slander: The utterance of defamatory statements injurious to the reputation of well-being of a person. A malicious statement or report.

Backbite: To speak spitefully or slanderously about a person. In most time behind a person's back.

Rail: To condemn or attack in bitter, harsh or abusive language.

Revile: To denounce with abusive language.

No matter if it's from media, magazine, or newspaper tabloids we seen these weapons in action and in full force. We also seen these weapons destroy churches, preachers and their families, destroy many families, ruin relationships, opportunities, visions, employments, goals, dreams, etc.

Let us be clear, these weapons are not biblical nor spiritual. They do not strengthen any household, empower any ministry, they do not bring life to any communities or lifestyles, nor do they represent love of any kind.

Let us secure this with scripture. Proverbs 11:9 says, 'With his mouth the godless man would destroy his neighbor, but by knowledge the righteous are delivered.' Life or Death, which one would you like to be labeled, no contest.

Now since we revealed the devils dirty work. Let's look at good, clean, refreshing words of good natures. We should be giving words of:

Encouraging: The action of giving some

support or hope.

Wisdom: The quality of having experience, knowledge, and good judgement, the quality of being wise.

Affirmation: emotional support or encouragement.

Love: A strong affection for another.

Comfort: A state of physical ease and freedom from pain or constant.

Inspiration: The process of being mentally stimulated to do or feel something, especially to do something creative.

You are a person full of life, a breath of fresh air that lasts, a love that never ends, a joy that lasts, and an inspiration that is everlasting. Remember that as you wear the color green. If you are a person of good virtue, green will look good on you, it will suit you well.

Chapter 5

BLACK

If you have been in the choir back in the days the natural color was black and white (white shirt, black bottoms. We will talk about white in the next chapter). In choir now in days it just be all black. Black is for our sins, it also means strength, authority, power.

Romans 3:9-12 says, 'What then? Are we Jews any better off? No, not at all. For we have already charged that all, both Jews and Greeks, are under sin, as it is written: "None is righteous, no, not one; no one understands; no one seeks for God. All have turned aside; together they have become worthless; no one does good, not even one."'

The bible is very clear in exposing the characteristics of Lucifer. His name means "Son of the Morning". He was considered to be the minister of music in heaven. He was also considered to be the most beautiful of all of the angels and was the first to be cast out of heaven.

So, I combine the terms the wages of sin, the ministry of music, and the color black. The purpose of Lucifer (also called Satan) in the music ministry of the church today is to destroy the morale of music ministry in churches everywhere. His attacks and techniques have been well known and for many years ministers of music have been well known to:

+ Be more concerned about the music

ministry only, not other ministries in the church.

- Trying to be more about popularity and not on purpose.

- Have so many egos and pitifulness.

- Creating a church within the music department.

Erasing the line between Pastor and a Minister of Music starts with these few things.

- Honor and Respect

- Having a humble heart

- Accountability and Responsibility

- Acknowledging all mighty God

"Acknowledging God"! That huge. Going back to the meaning of black, we are not worthy of his grace or mercy, nor are we worthy to worship and sing for him. But the biggest blessing when we acknowledge God is that knowing that our sins are forgiven.

2 Chronicles 7:14 says that if my people who are called by my name humble themselves and pray and seek my face and turn from their wicked ways, then I will hear from heaven and will forgive their sin and heal their land. Also in 1 John 1:8 If we say we have no sin, we deceive ourselves, and the truth is not in us.

So let us put it this way, tell the truth. Freedom starts with you being true to yourselves because that is where healing and relief starts. In fact, your strength is renewing so that you can walk and not be weary, run and not faint (Isaiah 40:31)

No matter what attire you wear, if you are a person that is downright and true, and then black is your color. It is just bait for a blessing of healing. It gets even better in the next chapter.

Chapter 6

What does forgiveness mean to you? Think about it for a second. There was a song I heard a long time ago, that if you wanted perfect people, he wouldn't use any one of us at all. If he wanted perfect churches, he wouldn't use any church at all.

In 2 Corinthians 5:17 Therefore, if anyone is in Christ, the new creation has come: The old has gone, the new is here! That's what the color White means. White is for our forgiveness. It means purity, goodness, safety, understanding, cleanness, faith, spiritually, (the color of snow and the color of our heaven is white).

In the article in the New York Times, Dee Poon, the head of retailing at Esquel decided to revitalize PYE, the company's own shirt label. According to the article she was selling what is feels is a perfect collection of white shirts. The prices started at $800 Hong Kong dollars, or about $100, and run up to $2,888 dollars for a white dress shirt in 200-threadcount fabric.

Just by reading the short article, I narrowed it down from the measure of our faith, to counting the cost, to paying the price. These are the things we deal with in our everyday lives.

In measuring of our faith Romans 12:3 tells us 'For by the grace given to me I say to everyone among you not to think of himself more highly than he ought to think, but to think with sober judgment, each according to the measure of faith that God has assigned.'

That is why it critical that we don't boast, talk or be boastful (years in the photography business I experienced it all the time). I don't even try to compete with other photographers. I have Jesus, the greater one, the prince of peace, the alpha and omega that lives inside of me I don't have to compete with nobody. **Bottom Line.**

Jeremiah 12:5 says, 'If you have raced with men on foot, and they have wearied you, how will you compete with horses? And if in a safe land you are so trusting, what will you do in the thicket of the Jordan?' With that said, if you have a talent and that you want God to bless it then put him first every day of your life.

Counting the Cost is very critical. According to Luke 14:28 it says, 'For which of you, desiring to build a tower, does not first sit down and count the cost, whether he has enough to complete it?' Having a talent is a gift but it's no joke. Sometimes it takes a lot of practice at the gym, a studio or a studying area.

The question is what are you willing to sacrifice? You might have to eliminate a lot of things and sadly a lot of people just to get it done. Are you willing to sacrifice or suffer for greatness? Leave the haters behind.

Luke 12:48 states: 'but the one who did not know, and did what deserved a beating, will receive a light beating. Everyone to whom much was given, of him, much will be required, and from him to whom they entrusted much, they will demand the more.' Get it? Much is given, much is required.

Paying the Price. In Galatians 3:13-14 it states, 'Christ redeemed us from the curse of the law by becoming a curse for us—for it is written, "Cursed is everyone who is hanged on a tree" — so that in Christ Jesus the blessing of Abraham might come to the Gentiles, so that we might receive the promised Spirit through faith.'

We don't have to measure ourselves, or count the cost, Jesus Christ already *Paid the Price* so that we can be stress free, worry free, set free, free to worship, free to walk with dignity, free from our sin, and the best freedom yet is forgiveness.

I am here to tell you that the color of White is clear, heaven is its goal, it is bold and beautiful, and its sky is the limit. Wear it.

Chapter 7

GOLD

Gold means wealth, success, and status. It is known as the color of achievement and triumph and also associated with higher ideas, wisdom, and enlightenment. It also inspires knowledge, spiritually and a deep understanding of the self and the soul. The one letter "L" in Gold stand for love.

John 3:16 says, 'For God so loved the world, that he gave his only Son, that whoever believes in him should not perish but have eternal life.'

Think of this the bible talks about us being precious than Gold. 1 Peter 1:7 says the tested genuineness of your faith—more precious than gold that perishes though it is tested by fire—may be found to result in praise and glory and honor at the revelation of Jesus Christ. Nevertheless, that is very crucial since we have already examined the meaning of Gold.

The Ark of the Covenant

1 Kings 10:18 talks about the king also made a great ivory throne and overlaid it with the finest gold. The building of the tabernacle was very important and every piece point to Christ and to his deity.

The holy of holies, the Ark of the Covenant was the symbolic of Jesus Humanity. Constructed out of acacia wood and overlaid with pure gold. The mercy seat was pure gold and the two cherubim, one of each side with wings outstretched. The lampstand was of pure gold and the table showbread, and the altar of incense constructed of acacia wood, overlaid with gold.

No matter how you put it, create it, or design it. We all know that Gold is valuable as it was to Jesus Christ and the Ark of the Covenant. In scripture, one of the wise men presented Jesus with a gift of Gold. A Gift befitting the king of kings that pointed to Jesus being the begotten Son of the living God.

Since we know how valuable, loving, and successful Gold is, it is not the importance of us wearing it. Are we designing each other with this valuable color? The worst thing that could ever happen is to look at everybody and everything as familiar. However, it can happen if we are not careful.

Some churches across the country are dealing with a lot is issues concerning the flock because people are not valuing each other. Going back to chapter 4 there is a lot of Gossip, Slander, Backbiting, Railing, Reviling and up to this day there are Rumors being spread all over the place.

It does not matter, verbal abuse, physical abuse, sexual abuse, damage to property, or even theft, we can prevent these things from happening everywhere if we value each other and show loyalty. Loyalty, Respect, and Appreciation are the main ingredients of Value.

Everything in life is a value. When you go to stores and shopping centers, you sometime see signs not to touch certain special items because it is of great value. You also can value your mother and father by taking time to go visit them and help them take care of certain needs.

The worst thing that we can do is to be a familiar or Complacent. Jesus Christ completed his mission for the forgiveness of our sins by dying on the cross. I believe that there was not one word in the bible that says Jesus was just a familiar or Complacent.

Most important not being Complacent. A complacent person is self – satisfied at things, easily satisfied with incremental growth and minor achievements, quick to offer all kinds of reasons about why they are not growing and cannot do anything new not planning wise as far as time, and importantly not coachable and full of pride.

Complacency not only divides any church, and any organization, but also kill any vision of any kind. Complacency is bad medicine. It does not play an important role. We cannot show value and loyalty to each other if we are complacent.

Think of somebody you can give encouragement too, something special you can do for somebody, someone to give a gift to, someone to inspire, someone to help. Think of that when you put on the attire filled with Gold. There is no familiar or Complacency in Gold. Remember you can be an inspiration designing unto others, as you would have the design unto you.

Chapter 8

The heart of God, The mind of Christ, and the blessing of the working of our hands. That defines the color of Turquoise. Turquoise is the first gemstone listed in the second row of the high priest breastplate. Its color stands for River of God, Sanctification, Healing, Refresh, Creativity.

Creativity is key, matter a fact it is very important. Let's go into the very beginning of Genesis which said in beginning God created the heavens and the earth, then he said let there be light and there was light.

Therefore, we know that the God that we serve is the God of creativity and with that comes patience. During my second year of marriage, I was rushing home one night to cook dinner for my wife who was on her way home.

Just when I thought I was the chef, I got a constructive criticism from my wife about the way I made it. First, she said that the meatballs were dry, and the rice was half-cooked. However, what she said was something that stuck in me. She said that if you want to do things with a lot of gratitude and from the heart.

No matter is doing a photo shoot or anything else, I do not like to rush things and I give honor to God through prayer before I work on anything.

The God we serve stressed the importance of patience.

✦ Ephesians 4:2- With all humility and gentleness, with patience, bearing with one another in love.

✦ Proverbs 25:15-With patience a ruler may be persuaded, and a soft tongue will break a bone.

✦ Psalms 37:7-Be still before the Lord and wait patiently for him; fret not yourself over the one who prospers in his way, over the man who carries out evil devices!

✦ Colossians 1:11- May you be strengthened with all power, according to his glorious might, for all endurance and patience with joy.

Anything you are doing, the first thing you want to do is slow down, study, ask questions, and take down some notes. It is wise to be patient and do it right than to rush and get it all wrong.

Let us talk about the mind of Christ. Jesus Christ. His home is in us. The Christ that can turn water into wine (John 2:1-11), made the blind man see and the lame man walk (Matthew 11:5), risen Lazarus from the dead (John 11:1-45 remember Lazarus was dead for 4 days), and at last pay the way for our salvation (Romans 5:6-10).

That is enough creativity right there and was only because Jesus Christ was the son of God. With that said, we must come to terms that we are what we create.

If you are, having a bad day is just because you spoke of it. If you keep saying that you are sick, than you are going to continue to be sick. The bottom line is that we cannot blame the devil or God for everything. We can create our own paths for blessings, and we can create our own paths for storms.

It is all about what we say, how we say it, and how we react. We can create our own problems because of a lack of purpose.

We can all create in a way that is pleasing to God. No matter is that boss on the job, that spouse; sometimes we just have to play their game. The game is called "Issues", because that is what people want "That Issue" and the only way to win the game is using God's creativity.

Turning the other cheek is a good example (Matthew 5:38-39). Be angry and yet do not sin is another example (Ephesians 4:26). In fact, there are time when silence is golden.

Many of you might have Turquoise in their closet. Always remember to always create great things and no matter what gifts you have through Christ love you can achieve more.

Chapter 9

BLUE

One of the colors that grew up with me for a long time. Blue has been empowering my life for a long time and is the inspiration for so many. Let us explain why.

The color Blue is a representation for being refreshed, restored, renewed, reset, reestablished, rethought, reinterpreted, and reimagine. I call Blue "the color of starting over. We all know that the color of water is blue. Water is an important source in our world today in so many proportions. However, baptism goes beyond the pure of water. Mark 1:8 says that I have baptized you with water, but he will baptize you with the Holy Spirit.

Baptism is the most important to the calling of the believer that has made a decision to follow Jesus Christ and give his or her life to him. Baptism is complete in three ways:

1. **Death**: Trading off the old wineskin for a new one is a complete purpose. Luke 9:23-24 says if anyone would come after me, he must deny himself and take up his cross daily and follow me. For whoever wants to save, his life will lose it, but whoever loses his life for me will save it.

Ask yourself, what you are willing to let go, to release, to surrender, to kick-to-the curve. Romans 12:2 says, 'do not be conformed to this world, but be ye transformed by the renewal of your mind, that by testing you may discern what the will of God is, what is good, acceptable, and perfect.'

It is nothing wrong to start thinking of positive things. When I had issues with my anger, my counselor told me to think about things which are free. I thought about that, we are paying the courts, the jails, and the attorneys, we are paying these court support social services. We need to think about freedom.

2. **<u>Burial</u>:** 2 Corinthians 5:1 says for we know that if the tent that is our earthly home is destroyed, we have a building from God, a house not made with hands, eternal in the heavens.

What is left in the dark has got to be brought to the light, what has died must be brought to life, what is lost must be found, and what was destroyed must be build up. Our bodies are not our own. We go down into the water as dead in the spirit, risen up alive in Christ.

3. **<u>Resurrection</u>**: The completed process. Resurrection is the concept of coming back to life after death. Romans 8:11 says that if the Spirit of him who raised Jesus from the dead dwells in you, he who raised Christ Jesus from the dead will also give life to your mortal bodies through his Spirit who dwells in you.

Prussian blue, also known as Berlin blue, is a dark blue pigment produced by oxidation of ferrous reagent, and its slightly different color stems from different impurities and particle size.

Here the important part; In medicine, orally administered Prussian blue is used as an antidote for certain kinds of heavy metal poisoning by thallium and radioactive isotopes of caesium.

The World Health Organization list Prussian blue as the most important medications needed in a basic health system.

But we don't even have issues with radiation, how about "hateration". In the dictionary, 'haterade' means excessive negativity, criticism, or resentment.

We all need a Prussian blue in our lives. Keep yourself separated against all negativity speaking in any proportions. Start being around positive influential people that is willing to put good seed into your spirit.

Better yet turn on some positive entertainment. All of the negative speaking and singing is not for you if you want to be encouraged.

We must talk up so that we can stay up.

I want to encourage you if you have any

hateration poisoning to be around virtue. To be refreshed by living water and to be equally connected with good fruit. Honoring each other, supporting each other, and continuing to bridging the gaps that divides us as a nation.

The purpose of blue is to renew you, restore you, and refresh you. Besides baptism, here is something to think of. The color of our water is blue, and it is a good thing. You should wear it.

Chapter 10

PURPLE

There was a meaning I came across "Women don't need to rehabilitate a man; he need to come assembled". After watching Tyler Perry's movie "Acrimony", I finally came to terms on one thing as a man. You do not need an alter for the wife cold as ice with an axe and one hand and a gun on another. I have to understand that whatever issue or need, I must be the protector, provider, and servant as Christ does the church. Prayer warriors not needed.

Before I get into the role of us as men, let us talk about the meaning for the color of Purple. Purple represents the royalty of the king of kings and the crown of life. James 1:12 says blessed is the man who remains steadfast under trial, for when he has stood the test he will receive the crown of life, which God has promised to those who love him.

The identity of a man is not possessions or tough talk or resources. It will he is able to stand the test. Will he be able to become a man of God first? It is never about money, cars, jewelry, fame; it is about having a heart of God and a mind of Christ, establishing a bible believing, spirit formed foundation that will bring all things into order. That is the way a man becomes assembled.

Please feel free to send me an email to share your perspective on, what is being a man all about, **jontuerice@gmail.com**. I would like to hear other perspectives. There are many perspectives. Here is my perspective.

<u>Identity</u>: Man vs. Thug. No contest. Being a male is a chance, being a man is a choice. The Identity of a man is true, straightforward, and accurate. He created the harvest, established spiritual foundations, and produces fruit in many proportions. It is all about how he dresses, how he articulates, and how he presents himself. Men, we have a lot of work to do.

<u>Character</u>: A teen locked up at a female juvenile detention center in Indiana, share her story about how is ended up there. She shares that coming up in life, she was not on that level of crime, but she wanted to see what was so good about the streets that her father could not come home at night. Enough said.

Without making excuses to having integrity issues, we have to question ourselves, how it affecting our children. When our children see us as men, what kind of Character do they see? An invisible dad, a dad that loves being cussed out, a dad with a nasty sense of humor, a dad that calls his gang the family, or a dad that loves going to jail.

There is no royalty or loyalty when the streets are becoming the father, and the question is not where the men are anymore. It is where the Men of Standard are.

Being a father is an important loyal occupation. An occupation that should not have to be asked to do, forced to do, but just do it. Satan do not want the royalty or loyalty to be the center of any family. That is why we as men need to pray for God to strengthen and empower us to live up to our expectation and continue to fight for the faith of our family.

Purple stand out as a feminine color and chosen by women worldwide, they do not mind wearing or taking the place of the royalty meaning of any house, they did it for years. However, I felt it is now time for the men to say, "Captain on the Bridge".

Chapter 11

Sapphire is a precious stone apparently of a bright-blue color (Exodus 24:10), the second stone in the second row of the high priest breastplate (Exodus 28:15-18), extremely precious (Job 28:16), and it was one of the precious stones that ornamented the King of Tyre (Ezekiel 28:13).

Sapphire meaning is wisdom, virtue, and faithfulness. The bible calls Sapphire as something very precious. Something that is precious is a substance of great value, not to be wasted or treated carelessly. There are people in our lives that are like Sapphire.

Aretha Franklin (the queen of soul) was a Sapphire, and she was a woman that had full of wisdom, virtue and full of faithfulness.

However, she was also precious (not to be wasted or treated carelessly) and that old song "RESPECT" was #1 on the Billboard chart, #5 of the Rolling Stone's list of the 500 greatest songs of all time and earned her two Grammy Awards.

However, the song itself is very important at times we are living in right now. I was able give an abbreviation to the word "RESPECT".

ROYAL: Isaiah 62:3 you shall be a crown of beauty in the hand of the Lord, and a royal diadem in the hand of your God.

EMPOWERED: Deuteronomy 31:6 be strong and courageous. Do not fear or be in dread of them, for it is the Lord your God who goes with you. He will not leave you or forsake you."

SERVANT: John 12:26 if anyone serves me, he must follow me; and where I am, there will my servant be also. If anyone serves me, the Father will honor him.

PURPOSE: Ephesians 1:11 in him we have obtained an inheritance, having been predestined according to the purpose of him who works all things according to the counsel of his will.

ENLIGHTEN: Proverbs 9:10-11, 'the fear of the Lord is the beginning of wisdom, and the knowledge of the Holy One is insight. For me your days will be multiplied, and years will be added to your life.'

CREATE: Exodus 35:35 He has filled them with skill to do every sort of work done by an engraver or by a designer or by an embroiderer in blue and purple and scarlet yarns and fine twined linen, or by a weaver--by any sort of workman or skilled designer.

TRUST: Proverbs 3:5-6 trust in the LORD with all your heart, and do not lean on your own understanding. In all your ways acknowledge him, and he will make straight your paths.

A person that shows Respect is a Royal Empowered Servant with a Purpose to Enlighten and Create Trust. It is a person that is willing to turn competitiveness into community. In order to have the Respect you must give the Respect.

"Rivalry, Jealousy, and Cattiness are the worst things woman do to each other. Getting over it and getting together is the key to success for all of us." – Ashley Graham. Plus Size Model.

Without respect, everybody loses, and nobody wins. Remember much is given, much is required. Respect goes long ways. The late Minister Maxine Walker said something a long time ago that touched be today. She said that "You May not Like Me, You May not Love me, but you must respect me."

Respect determines how faithful we are, how much virtue we have and how wise we can be. You are a Sapphire person, a person that is precious when you are a person of Respect. Wear it! Wear it! Wear it!

Chapter 12

BROWN

Brown is known as the healing process of God. The healing process starts with having a solid foundation or stability. It also starts with honesty and commitment.

Numbers 15:38-41 Speak to the people of Israel and tell them to make tassels on the corners of their garments throughout their generations, and to put a cord of blue on the tassel of each corner. And it shall be a tassel for you to look at and remember all the commandments of the Lord, to do them, not to follow after your own heart and your own eyes, which you are inclined to whore after. So, you shall remember and do all my commandments, and be holy to your God. I am the Lord your God, who brought you out of the land of Egypt to be your God: I am the Lord your God."

It also starts with coming to terms with the fact that there are things we need to become correct and to change. Matthew 13:16-17 says blessed are your eyes, for they see, and your ears, for they hear. For truly, I say to you, many prophets and righteous people longed to see what you see, and did not see it, and to hear what you hear, and did not hear it.

It's important that in all we getting we must get understanding (Proverbs 4:7). It all starts with where we sow our seeds into as well Matthew 13:18-23 breaks it down in four kinds of grounds on where the seeds falls on and the outcome it has.

Path: Anyone hears the word of the kingdom and does not understand it the evil comes and snatches away what has been sown in his heart. This is what was sown along the path. People like these are often in church but more in the world plenty of the time.

Rocky: This is the one who hears the word and immediately receives it with joy, yet he has no root in himself but endures for a while and when tribulation or persecution arises on account of the word, immediately he falls away.

These people are the ones that need to have morning devotions every day. They must be reminded of who they are and who they serve. The point is to not make tribulations your God.

Thorns: This is the one who hears the word, but the cares of the world and the deceitfulness of riches choke the word, and it proves unfruitful.

These people need to start cutting off soul ties, generational curses, and so many other unwelcoming spirits. Just because it looks good doesn't mean that its healthy for you.

Good: This is the one who hears the word and understands it. He indeed bears fruit and yields in one case a hundredfold, in another sixty, and another thirty.

These people not only take God seriously, but they expect an overflowing anointing of the holy spirit.

In fact, which is where the healing begins. It starts with getting things in order. It starts with placing our feet on solid ground and not allowing anything that is ungodly and not according to the word of God.

Before you wear that brown attire, please understanding that anybody can end up anywhere, but you are going to end up somewhere on purpose. I hope that somewhere is good ground.

Chapter 13

SILVER

Silver gives representation of one of the most valuable and important things, the meaning "PURITY". Staying pure is the most important mission is this walk of faith. It is very critical that teens need to know the importance of purity.

Staying Pure in a hyper-sexualized word is important. The idea is to planning a strategy for a strong foundation. I came up with these four things.

1. Hearing the truth- John 8: 31-32 So Jesus said to the Jews who had believed him, "If you abide in my word, you are

truly my disciples, and you will know the truth, and the truth will set you free.

2. Growing Faith- Romans 10:17 so faith comes from hearing, and hearing through the word of Christ.

3. Strengthen yourself to live for Christ- Isaiah 40:31 but they who wait for the Lord shall renew their strength; they shall mount up with wings like eagles; they shall run and not be weary; they shall walk and not faint.

4. Growing Purity and living for him- 1 Timothy 4:12 Let no one despise you for your youth, but set the believers an example in speech, in conduct, in love, in faith, in purity.

A person that first hears the truth, which is the word of God, will increase his or her faith through the Baptism of the Hold Spirit. After that, the person will continue to strengthen his or her foundation and walk boldly. That person will also continue to walk with Purity.

A 2017 published book, "A New Model" by author and plus size model, Ashley Graham, explains that when it comes to "My Vagina," great power comes great responsibility. "Don't fall into the trap of sacrificing your self-esteem for affection and acceptance."

Adolescence is defined as a person that is no longer a child but not yet an adult. (Teenagers). That word is very critical. It is critical now more than ever that teenagers are planted with good seeds and are equally yoked with good law-abiding citizens.

Romans 12:1 says, 'I appeal to you therefore, brothers, by the mercies of God, to present your bodies as a living sacrifice, holy and acceptable to God, which is your spiritual worship. '

Also, in 1 Corinthians 6:19-20 it says, 'You not know that your body is a temple of the Holy Spirit within you, whom you have from God? You are not your own, for you were bought with a price. So, glorify God in your body.'

Just because you came out of your mother's womb doesn't mean that your body belongs to you. Christ gave his life and paid the price so that you can have life and have it more abundantly (John 10:10).

Teenagers, especially girls, need to hear that their bodies are good and beautiful. Romans 12:2 do not be conformed to this world, but be transformed by the renewal of your mind, that by testing you may discern what the will of God is, what is good, acceptable, and perfect.

Knowing what is and what is not

acceptable is the key because not everything is acceptable. Teenagers, both girls and boys need parents to understand their world. Let us understand that Facebook, Twitter, Snap Chat, Instagram, and all crazy social media websites that is out there today should not be the solid foundation of our youth.

I would like to freestyle paraphrase in my words, Luke 14:26-27, just a little, "If anyone comes to me and does not hate his own Facebook site, Instagram site, even their Twitter site, or any other site, he cannot be my disciple. Whoever does not bear his own cross and come after me cannot be my disciple. Enough Said.

From purity jewelry to attire. I was wondering about the wonderful benefit of wearing silver. It helps with internal heat regulation and circulation. It also shown improvements in energy levels and balance in moods after wearing silver. It also improves circulation and overall body temperature balance and help maintain cleanliness and immunity. That is Purity.

Chapter 14

PINK

The color of Pink symbolizes a right relationship with God through Heart of Flesh (Ezekiel 11:19), Joy (Psalms 32:1, Nehemiah 8:10), and Passion for Jesus (Song of Solomon 1:2). Again, much is given, much is required. Here is the one thing we need to do to be in that right relationship. That thing is to T.U.R.N.

TRUST: Ezekiel 11:19 says I will give them one heart, and a new spirit I will put within them. I will remove the heart of stone from their flesh and give them a heart of flesh.

UNDERSTANDING: Proverbs 3:5-6 says, 'Trust in the Lord with all your heart, and do not lean on your own understanding. In all your ways, acknowledge him, and he will make straight your paths.'

REPENT: Acts 2:38 says "Repent and be baptized every one of you in the name of Jesus Christ for the forgiveness of your sins, and you will receive the gift of the Holy Spirit.

NEW: 2 Corinthians 5:17 says Therefore, if anyone is in Christ, he is a new creation. The old has passed away; behold, the new has come.

Let me share if you love someone what would you do to show that you love him or her. Love does not have it measurements nor limitations. It can bless someone, heal someone, change or empower someone's life 1 Corinthians 13:4-7 says Love is patient and kind; love does not envy or boast; it is not arrogant or rude. It does not insist on its own way; it is not irritable or resentful; it does not rejoice at wrongdoing but rejoices with the truth. Love bears all things, believes all things, hopes all things, and endures all things.

Also in 1 Corinthians 13:3 it says, 'If I give away all I have, and if I deliver up my body to be burned, but have not love, I gain nothing.'

I was thinking about so many people that claims they are gifted and talented in their profession. Not to judge them but was wondering do they applied love in what they are doing. For example, when I do photo shoots, I see myself as being an inspiration to somebody. That goes beyond comparing, competition or pride.

Jesus went to Calvary to save a wretch like you and me. That is love. Love that has and will last forever and only if shared can save or bless a life. Wearing it in one thing sharing it is another. Remember Design unto others as you would have them design unto you.

Chapter 15

BUILD YOUR OWN IMAGE

Ssehura, more known by her European given name Sarah Baartman, was a <u>Khoikhoi</u> woman who spent her childhood and teenage years on Dutch European farms.

She was encouraged by a free black slave trader named Peter Cesars. She spent two years working in households, as a washerwoman and a nursemaid for Caesar and another Dutch man.

She was later asked by Cesars brother Hendrik to exhibit her at the city hospital in exchange for cash. She was later asked to be on display in Europe.

From then as a woman named "Hottest Venus" that had a huge body shape especially around the gluteal regions she was presented on many occasions from slave traders to highly rich members. Member that would continue to trade her off to others for higher profits in exhibits.

I asked how a woman that was so special died at such young age (26). Then as I learn the story of Sarah Baartman, we have to talked about not only the epitome of racist colonial exploitation and of the commodification of the dehumanization of Black women today, but what is it doing to the word "Model". It's terrible that our character is being determined by those to either want to take advantage of it or dehumanize it.

The purpose of the book of John was to communicate the truths about Christ to Christians of Hellenistic background.

In the book of John 3:28 if says You are witnesses that I said, "I'm not the Messiah, but I've been sent ahead of him." You get the first part of it. John said that you are witnesses that I said I am not the Messiah. Many tried to tell John the Baptist that he was the messiah but only John knew who he was.

I made a commitment that I don't have to be like anybody. I don't have to be popular to fulfill my sense of purpose. I don't have to compromise nor betray myself. My character that Christ gave me is honorable and I desire to have.

Are you trying to get to your destination using the wrong routes, creating short cuts to get there, and using the cheapest way of method just to complete the mission?

We forgot this important word "Integrity". It's all about being honest and having strong moral principles. A person with integrity behaves ethically and does the right thing, even behind closed doors. It's about being true to yourself. It's all about knowing who you are.

Sadly, we have let people we never met in modern life determine that for us. To them its ok to be out of purpose and out of touch to gain fame or have more profit. Ask yourself, what goodness does that bring?

Do we have to turn public schools into private schools so our students are in uniform just so their hearts and minds are protected? Is employers discipline their employees over dress code is in violation of their rights?

Are you honest with yourself with what you wear, or do you just want to prove a point, to get fame, or get attention? Neither way you faking. You are not being true to yourself wearing proactive clothing, and other attire that brings no purpose.

If you are in desperate need to have buttock augmentations and breast enhancements, then you are not being true to yourself. You are a slave to believing what you feel and how you feel except acknowledging what is real.

Angela Renée White (known as Blac Chyna) expressed that it was time to be real with herself. Several enhancements and implants, so many lawsuits, and so many unhealthy relationships I know the feeling.

It was time for Blac Chyna to stop being a slave to popularly and start to have a sense of purpose. She also stated that she had deleted her OnlyFans account, while also reversing some of her plastic surgery and removing her occultic tattoos.

I am so happy to see her walking with the Lord. That means that see is set free from the junk and unhealthy spirits that surround her. She got a new image and a brighter outlook while she still keeping her sass.

So, while you are doing an evaluation on yourself already. Let's talk about building an image that is God's approved. It is going to start with acknowledging Ephesians 6:10-17. Yes, the armor of God. We need it to guard our beliefs, what we stand for and the purpose thereof.

So, let's explore what it means to put on the armor of God.

- <u>The Belt of Truth</u>- The point is holding it all together. Knowing that the truth shall set you free (John 8:44) and acknowledging our personal commitment to God by holding truth. Truth to living a life that is upright, transparent, and without deceit.

✚ <u>Breastplate of Righteousness</u> – Is Christ righteousness, not our own righteousness. The breastplate covers the heart and other vital organs. The Bible says, "Keep your heart with all diligence, for out of it spring the issues of life" (Proverbs 4:23).

✚ That is what Christ's righteousness does for you. It protects you against all of Satan's accusations and charges. This righteousness is not made up of the good deeds you do. The Bible is clear that none of us are righteous in ourselves (Romans 3:10).

- Shoes of the Gospel – So you are marching into battle. Shall you wear high heels?

As soldiers of Christ, we must put on "gospel shoes" that will allow us to march wherever our Lord leads. The apostle John says, "He who says he abides in Him [Jesus] ought himself also to walk just as He [Jesus] walked" (1 John 2:6).

Jesus said, "My sheep hear My voice, . . . and they follow Me" (John 10:27). Satan will try to place obstacles in our path, but in Jesus' strength we can walk forward, following our Lord, obeying Him, and advancing the gospel.

- Shield of Faith - This faith is not something that comes from within us. It is God's gift to us. He gives each of us a measure of faith (Romans 12:3). Then as we walk with Him, that faith grows and develops until it becomes a shield, protecting us and allowing us to live a victorious life in Christ.

✚ <u>Helmet of Salvation</u> - The helmet protects the head—perhaps the most vital part of the body since it is the seat of thought and the mind. When we have a sure knowledge of our salvation, we will not be moved by Satan's deceptions. When we are certain that we are in Christ with our sins forgiven, we will have a peace that nothing can disturb.

Can we be certain of our salvation? Can we be sure?

Yes. "If we confess our sins, He [Jesus] is faithful and just to forgive us our sins and to cleanse us from all unrighteousness" (1

John 1:9). "God has given us eternal life, and this life is in His Son. He who has the Son has life" (1 John 5:11, 12).

- <u>Sword of the Spirit</u> - The sword of the spirit is the only weapon of offense listed in the armor of God. All the other parts are defensive in nature.
- God's Word the Bible is described as "living and powerful, sharper than any two-edged sword" (Hebrews 4:12). Jesus used this weapon when Satan was tempting Him in the wilderness.
- To each of Satan's efforts to lead Him into sin, Jesus replied, "it is written...." and proceeded to quote the Scriptures in order to destroy Satan's temptations. God's Word is truth (John 17:17). That is why it is so powerful.

✚ That is why it is so important that we study the Bible and become familiar with its truths and its power.

David wrote, "Your word is a lamp to my feet and a light to my path" (Psalm 119:105). The sword of God's Word both protects us and destroys our enemy—the devil and his temptations.

Every color mentioned and expressed in this book, I guarantee that it will refresh, empower, enlighten, uplift, excite, and it will bring new awakening.

But wait where was just one only color that is great with this chapter "Blue". That is the color that represents honesty and integrity. It is one of the most common colors of choice, because it's the most trustworthy.

It communicates wisdom, freedom,

loyalty, and honesty. Is that you, are you willing to wear and be truthful to yourself so that you can be a beacon to those you surround yourself around and you don't have to be bound by anything or anybody.

Go ahead, build your own brand, build your own image but build it with honesty, integrity and the way God wants it to be. Stay true to you and let nobody take that away from you.

Thank You For The Support!

THE
INSPIRATION
FASHION
Colors of Jesus' Soul